# Dimensions of Spiritual Breakthrough

A Spirit Life Training supplement

Timothy Jorgensen

# Dimensions of Spiritual Breakthrough

A Spirit Life Training Supplement

Timothy Jorgensen

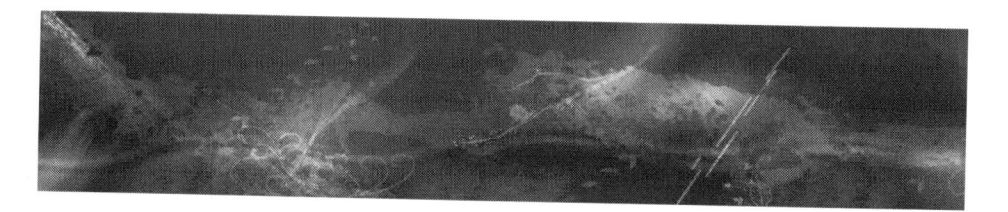

**How to use this book:**

This book is structured in a particular way in order to be functional for the reader.

<u>The title</u> is given as a concise phrase concerning what to believe for, so that aspect of Spiritual Breakthrough will become operational in your life. (Matt 8:13)

<u>The scriptures</u> are given as a Word-base for why we have the right to believe for this to come to pass in our life. By these precious promises we become partakers of the divine nature. (2 Pet.1:4)

The 'What This Means' portion goes into more depth of what this aspect of Spiritual Breakthrough will look like in our lives. This is important as it activates the imagination and intellect to be able to more fully participate in your planned adventures in this life of the spirit. However, what has been meditated and written out for you is not complete, but it is a blueprint and a platform for you to take it to another level of practicality for your life.

Breakthroughs do not come by desire alone, but by taking personal responsibility to diligently apply principles in your everyday environment.

For this reason, after each section, there are practical questions to challenge you to release and experience these dimensions of Spiritual Breakthrough. Do not gloss over each one and the Holy Spirit will help you to make everything personal to your unique situations. The wonderful thing is this: as your situations change from month to month, or year to year, these tools will once again become fresh as they can be applied in dynamic new ways for you. As you transform, your tests and challenges morph accordingly, and become new stepping-stones to a greater revealing of the Christ in you. The Holy Spirit will then help you see how these areas of breakthrough can be applied in a new way for that stage of your transformation. This book will be useful for many years to come!

## Table of Contents

1. God Consciousness at all Times
2. Clarity of Vision
3. Able to Receive Greater Insight and Perception
4. Greater Flow of Revelation
5. Build Greater Capacity
6. Great Strength in Spirit and Voice
7. Spiritual Buoyancy

# God consciousness at all times

"For you are the temple of the Living God. As God has said *"I will dwell in them and walk among them, I will be their God and they shall be My people."* (2Cor.6:16)

## WHAT THIS MEANS:

Wherever you may go, you have an acute consciousness that God is in you and around you. The value of this is that when you have this consciousness, you have a sensitivity to ask Him questions, believe He will hear and act the moment you ask, and your entire conduct will be governed in the conscious understanding that you abide under His shadow. The promises of Psalm 91 only belong to those who have this consciousness.

Apart from this awareness, when crisis hits, you feel guilty and distant from Him- even though that may not be the case at all. Not having this awareness will actually cripple your ability to act on the truth that Christ lives in you and is your very present help in the time of need.

When you can have this breakthrough where your mind and spirit have a constant unshakable 'knowing' that He is in and surrounding you, this mental and spiritual sensitivity will unlock a multitude of changes in your life.

First, you will have a <u>new boldness</u> about you. You can say like Elijah- *"..as the Lord God lives, before Whom I stand..."* You know your position in His very Presence, and realize that you cannot be moved from that place.

Next, you will also have a <u>new character</u> in you. When we abide in the light, there is no darkness, there is no secrecy, there is no hiding. DL Moody once stated *"Character is what a man is in the dark."* When one thinks no one is looking, that is where we find the character of a person. This God consciousness changes all that. In fact, <u>God consciousness revolutionizes our *conscience*</u>. Our conscience continually *'bears witness in the Holy Spirit'* (Acts 23:1, Rom.9:1) We have a constantly activated guidance system, with the Helper standing by, to make sure we live out everything we know is right to do. People suffer shipwreck because they do not hold onto this good conscience and faith. God consciousness removes this from ever becoming an issue in any area of your life. What safety this provides for us! I submit this observation to you, that every minister who has had moral failures has lost his/her sense of God consciousness a long time ago.

Along with this benefit to our character, this <u>new sensitivity increases our precision in God's guidance for us</u>. When God knows our sensitivity is increased, He can guide us much quicker throughout our lives and decision-making processes.

In terms of <u>believing for the miraculous</u>, this God consciousness is a prerequisite. As a practical exercise, John G. Lake made a habit of walking over to his mirror, pointing to it as if to another person and saying , "*God lives in that man in that suit of clothes. And where that suit of clothes goes, God goes.*" Another term for this habit is being 'God-inside minded.' From this declaration, we see a catalyst for successful miracle ministries and a full operation of the gifts of the Holy Spirit.

At the same time, a fresh God consciousness will also produce a <u>new love</u> in your life. These fruits of the Holy Spirit are the result of knowing as He surrounds you, He surrounds you with a love that is penetrating, and mercy, grace and truth that are everlasting. It changes how you react, and changes how you see situations. This will also give you an inner security in the midst of trials and persecution that will inspire songs of deliverance. How is it really possible to love your enemies and bless those who persecute you? You are overflowing with delight in something that no one could take away from you. This consciousness inspired these words at the pinnacle of Romans 8:31-38

*"What then shall we say to these things? If God is for us, who can be against us? He who did not spare His own Son, but delivered Him up for us all, how shall He not with Him also freely give us all things? Who shall bring a charge against God's elect? It is God who justifies. Who is he who condemns? It is Christ who died, and furthermore is also risen, who is even at the right hand of God, who also makes intercession for us."*

"Who shall separate us from the love of Christ? Shall tribulation, or distress, or persecution, or famine, or nakedness, or peril, or sword? As it is written: 'For Your sake we are killed all day long; We are accounted as sheep for the slaughter.' Yet in all these things we are more than conquerors through Him who loved us. For I am persuaded that neither death nor life, nor angels nor principalities nor powers, nor things present nor things to come, nor height nor depth, nor any other created thing, shall be able to separate us from the love of God which is in Christ Jesus our Lord."

You smile in the face of adversity, because you are conscious of Him, and He is Love, and Love never fails.

The ripple effects of this dimension of spiritual breakthrough will go on and on!

**Challenge Questions:**

In believing and expecting this spiritual breakthrough dimension of God consciousness, note situations where you have experienced:

**Boldness because of God Consciousness**

_____
_____
_____
_____
_____
_____

**New Character Changes because of God Consciousness**

_____
_____
_____
_____
_____
_____

**Increased Precision in God's Guidance because of God Consciousness**

_____
_____
_____
_____
_____
_____
_____

**Events of the Miraculous because of God Consciousness**

_____
_____
_____
_____
_____
_____
_____


**Stronger sense of God's Love to and through you because of God Consciousness**

_____
_____
_____
_____
_____
_____
_____

# Clarity of Vision; your spirit is sharp, Able to discern other spirits, Can feel out a situation

"...the utterance of the man whose eyes are opened; the utterance of him who hears the words of God and knows the knowledge of the Most High, who sees the vision of the Almighty..."
(Num.24:15-16)

"But the anointing which you have received from Him abides in you, and you do not need that anyone teach you; but as the same anointing teaches you concerning all things, and is true, and not a lie, and just as it has taught you, you will abide in Him."
(1 John 2:27)

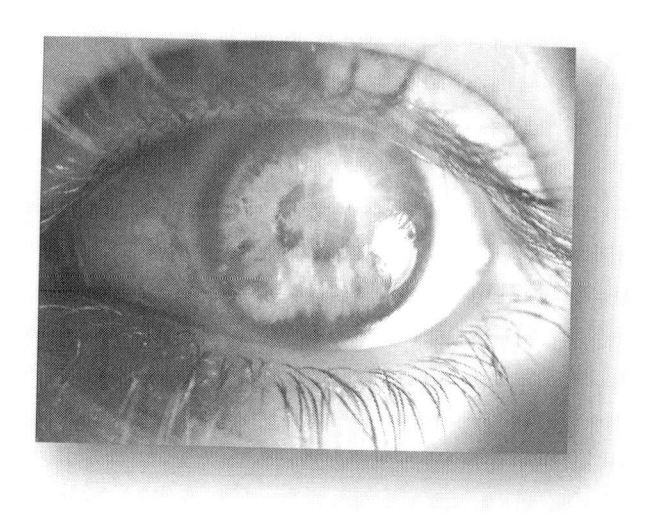

## What This Means:

In Ephesians chapter 1, after the apostle Paul declares our spiritual position in Christ, he introduces a very important prayer that makes a request that the eyes of our spiritual understanding be opened on three different levels. I will not get into those levels here, but the question I want to ask is: What are our spiritual eyes? Simple, it is what our spirit sees. But sometimes these eyes can be dim because of how we depend on natural sight and understanding of the body and soul more than the candle of the Lord- our spirit. When our spirit sees things, it sees them from God's point of view, and things are not always as they first appear. A good situation could actually look bad, and a bad situation could actually look good at first. We cannot judge according to natural appearance, but by what our spirit can see. We can enter a room and see what is going on spiritually. People call this 'prophetic' but really, this is simply a basic use of your recreated spirits eyesight. What we see in the natural can simply be a puppet stage, but our spirits can see who/what is behind the curtain, and what their intentions are.

When we start walking in this aspect of spiritual breakthrough, our spiritual senses will be heightened, and what a difference it will make! Imagine someone that is newly no longer blind, or no longer deaf- a whole new world is now available. Be prepared, this will change so much about your habits, relationships and even your personality. This will also cause you to be a new spiritual weapon in God's army. Balaam was hired as a spiritual mercenary because of what he could do because of what he could hear and see. This is another area you need to be prepared about, as this can open up another level of temptation to abuse what you hear and see for your own benefit rather than for the building up of others and the kingdom. Peter, Jude and John (Jesus actually) all warn that the attitude and dangers of Balaam still exist in our era and try to hang out around the church.

**Challenge Questions:**

In believing and expecting this spiritual breakthrough dimension of Clarity of Vision, note situations where you have experienced:

New 'things' (behind the scenes workings, spiritual beings, inner visions, flashes of symbolic images, etc) you have been able to see with the eyes of your spirit, and the situation(s) in which you have seen them.

1. _____
   _____
   _____
   _____
   _____

2. _____
   _____
   _____
   _____
   _____

3. _____
   _____
   _____
   _____
   _____

New understandings (supernatural details, discernment of a person's nature and issues/influences, hearing a word spoken from the Spirit, etc) you have been able to hear or just 'know' with the ears or understanding of your spirit, and the situation(s) in which you have received this.

1. _____
_____
_____
_____
_____

2. _____
_____
_____
_____
_____

3. _____
_____
_____
_____
_____

# Able to Receive Greater Insight and Perception

"And immediately, when Jesus perceived in His spirit that they reasoned thus within themselves, He said to them..." (Mark 2:8)

"The Lord God has opened my ear; and I was not rebellious, nor did I turn away." (Isa.50:5)

## WHAT THIS MEANS:

Back to Ephesians chapter 1, Paul does not just pray for spiritual eyes to be opened, he prays that the eyes of our *understanding* to be enlightened. It is good to see something, but it is more important to understand the fuller picture about what you see and what to do about it. This takes insight and perception. This element of spiritual breakthrough gives the understanding about the situation you now see and the discernment to know what to say.

Even more important – this insight will give you exactly what you need to know. You get the word for the moment, in order to act for the moment. Jesus perceived thoughts as if they were spoken in order to address the exact issue at hand. Paul perceived a strategy of how to speak and act in the midst of a pack of religious wolves in Acts 23. Paul also perceived in his spirit the end of the situation when he was taken on a Roman galley ship in Acts 27, but he also had the insight to know how to act to improve the situation. This fluidity of spiritual sensitivity, insight and perception takes the illusion of inevitability out of the prophetic. We have insight to act based on what our spirit sees and the understanding that the Spirit of God gives us. This will cause spiritual changes in the potential outcome, which will ultimately change the end outcome's manifestation.

**Challenge Questions:**

In believing and expecting this spiritual breakthrough dimension of receiving greater insight and perception, note situations where you have experienced:

Perception of the thoughts and reasoning of others- knew it by the spirit.

1._____
_____
_____
_____

2._____
_____
_____
_____

3._____
_____
_____
_____

Times where you were able to turn a prophetic word or insight around because of your spiritual wisdom in how you responded to that word.

1._____
_____
_____
_____

2._____
_____
_____
_____

3._____
_____
_____
_____

**Times you were able to perceive a strategy by the spirit, and understand how it would play out before it actually happened.**

1._____
_____
_____
_____

2._____
_____
_____
_____

3._____
_____
_____
_____

# Greater flow of Revelation

"Jesus answered and said to him, 'Because I said to you, 'I saw you under the fig tree,' do you believe? You will see greater things than these... Most assuredly, I say to you, hereafter you shall see heaven open and the angels of God ascending and descending upon the Son of Man"  (John 1:50-51)

"Blessed are you...for flesh and blood has not revealed this to you, but My Father who is in heaven...and I will give you the keys of the kingdom of heaven, and whatever you bind on earth will be bound in heaven, and whatever you loose on earth will be loosed in heaven." (Matt.16:17,19)

## What This Means:

One of the most difficult principles for us to grasp is the Luke 16:10 factor.

*"He who is faithful in what is least is faithful also in much; and he who is unjust in what is least is unjust also in much."* We want more of Christ's thoughts, character and power to manifest through our lives. However, we often do not see the necessity of each situation to leverage our faithfulness so that more of what has been promised, can be released and experienced.

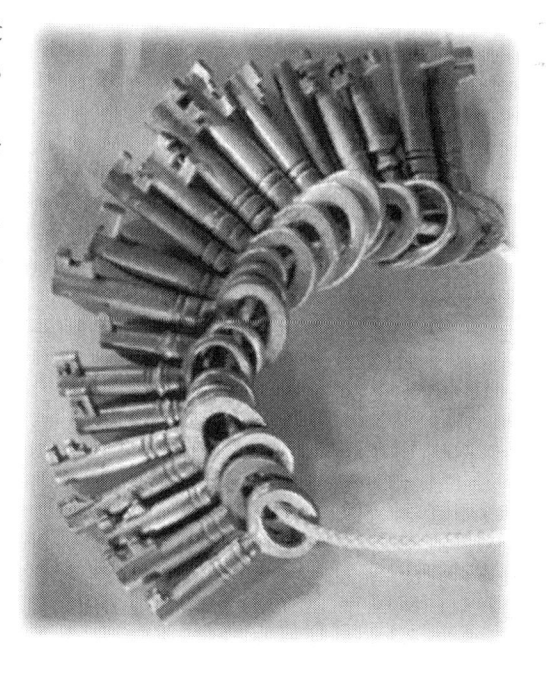

In each of these above situations, a spiritual transaction took place that leveraged that person to see another world of opportunity. Nathanael believed a simple prophetic word from Jesus, and saw into the character of Jesus through that word and called Him King and the Son of God. Because of this faithfulness to the word he received, Jesus pointed out how that ready faith that he used was going to leverage him to much greater revelations of spiritual realities. When Peter was asked who he thought Jesus was, Peter answered the same as Nathanael and declared Jesus to be the Son of the Living God. Strangely, Jesus did not celebrate the correct answer, *but the process* by which he arrived at the answer! Why? Again He was highlighting the fact that when someone counts a word from Heaven (Logos or Rhema) as precious, that character to be faithful to the heavenly Word will leverage any Word from Heaven to be used as a key to release or lock up other spiritual activity.

Again, going back to the prayer in Ephesians 1:15-23, it was only AFTER Paul knew that the believers had been solid in their faith in the Lord Jesus, and love for their brethren, that he took it to another level to pray that a fresh release of the Spirit of Wisdom and Revelation would be given to them. And as we look to the end of verse 23 we really can see how 'faithful over little' will surely translate into 'ruler over much!'

When we are faithful to use and speak what spiritual realities from God that we see and hear, this will break us through to new levels of spiritual revelations, activities and effectiveness. Jesus wants us to be constantly increasing in fruitfulness. All of Heaven is giving us a green light, and ready to flood us with increasing revelation that we <u>need</u> to know. All that is withholding is our capacity to be faithful to what we have already received and know. Let's believe for faithfulness to the heavenly vision/word to become our passion(Acts 26:19)- and nothing could then stop this aspect of spiritual breakthrough from breaking forth.

**Challenge Questions:**

In believing and expecting this spiritual breakthrough dimension of receiving a greater flow of revelation, note situations where you have experienced:

Revelations of the truths of God, and how your faithfulness to speak and act on them has opened up new revelations leading to new experiences and understandings.

1._____
_____
_____
_____

2._____
_____
_____
_____

3._____
_____
_____
_____

What 'keys of the kingdom' are you confident you know, possess, and can use, resulting in binding and loosing of spiritual events in people's lives?

1._____
_____
_____
_____

2._____
_____
_____
_____

3._____
_____
_____
_____

# Your spirit is able to stretch out and build great capacity into it

"You are of God, little children, and have overcome them, because He who is in you is greater than he who is in the world." (1 John4:4)

"Enlarge the place of your tent, and let them stretch out the curtains of your habitations; Do not spare; Lengthen your cords, and strengthen your stakes. For you shall expand to the right hand and to the left, and your descendants will inherit the nations, and make the desolate cities inhabited." (Isa.54:2-3)

## WHAT THIS MEANS:

We are a lot bigger than we first appear! And the question is, if 1 John 4:4 is true, then why is our world domination not yet tangibly experienced? There could be a number of answers to this, but we must come to a place where every roadblock is taken out of the way until the Spirit of Christ that lives in us, covers the earth with His dominion. This is our portion, and we must experience it.

We know we are the temple of the Holy Spirit, but that does not mean that the Holy Spirit must be caged and limited to only act within the vicinity of the physical temple! When we understand that the Holy Spirit is our helper, and our spirit can extend to any place our mind will allow it to go, the challenge will be to have the capacity to keep the ground we extend our spirit to by faith. Paul hinted of this capacity in (1Cor.5:4-5) This takes focus and a peace-ruled mind. It cannot be done if one is selfish, worried, or double-minded in doubtfulness. Spiritual capacity cannot survive in that environment.

To help us, this verse from Isaiah 54 is a great picture of our capacity to spread our 'shadow' (Acts5:15). However, it first takes a determination to have this spiritual breakthrough to enlarge, and stretch out our spiritual territory. You must be bigger! Your spirit must touch, effect, infiltrate, and begin to captivate those within the room... the building... the area.... the city.... the territory.... the nation.... the world.... All for the cause of Christ. Everything becomes subservient to the Him in you. Next, we must have our cords lengthened and our stakes strengthened so every work and victory done by our spiritual capacity is not unraveled by our lacking to solidify what we have done. Our actions, words and faith line up with what our spirit has accomplished. Our victory must be perpetual, not temporary, so again, faithfulness to what we have received continues to establish our rulership. Lastly, we establish good things in the environment. The desert blossoms as a rose- and you begin to create people who perpetuate the good work you started.

What an amazing aspect of spiritual breakthrough is available to us in this!

**Challenge Questions:**

In believing and expecting this spiritual breakthrough dimension of being able to stretch your spirit and receive a greater capacity, note instances where you have experienced:

Greater distances where you have been able to impact situations with your spirit. Where previously you felt you had to be in a certain proximity, but now you can handle more situations without being limited by your physical body.

1._____
_____
_____
_____

2._____
_____
_____
_____

3._____
_____
_____
_____

**Greater abilities to keep victories won, and ground gained because of your spirit's ability to 'plant stakes in the ground' in that situation.**

1._____
_____
_____
_____

2._____
_____
_____
_____

3._____
_____
_____
_____

# Great strength in spirit and voice

"...that He would grant you, according to the riches of His glory, <u>to be strengthened with might through His Spirit in the inner man</u>... now to Him who is able to do exceedingly abundantly above all we ask or think, according to the power that works in us..." (Eph.3:16,20)

"...and he who has My Word, let him speak My Word faithfully...Is not My Word like a fire?" says the LORD, "And like a hammer that breaks the rock in pieces?"
(Jer.23:28-29)

"Most assuredly, I say to you, the hour is coming, and now is, when the dead shall hear the Voice of the son of God; and those who hear shall live." (John 5:25)

## WHAT THIS MEANS:

In the first prayer of Ephesians chapter 1, Paul prays for spiritual sight and revelation for the believers. In this second prayer of Ephesians 3 he takes it to another level by asking for spiritual strength and power to manifest in them. This strengthening of the spirit is pictured as a dormant capacity within these believers, and Paul is praying that they would get the kickstart from the Spirit of God within, so they will start to grasp this fullness of God in them through operational faith and experiential love.

This is interesting to me- why Paul would put the request concerning power, before the request concerning love? Same thing when Paul says to Timothy that he was not given a spirit of fear but of power, love, and a sound mind. (2 Tim.1:7) Again, power is put first. It seems to me, that it is when the Spirit's power is increased, it can then bring to life this love that is rooted in us through Christ. Power becomes a vehicle to express a nature.

Jesus said that out of the abundance of the heart, the mouth will speak. Words carry the character of the heart. But what carries the words? <u>The voice is the vehicle</u>. Peter said this **"If anyone speaks, let him speak as the oracles of God."** (1 Peter 4:11a) It's not just *what* you say, it is HOW ('the way') you say it that releases the ability, glory, and dominion of God! Words carry knowledge, but a VOICE carries a spirit. It is important to *discern* voices to protect yourself and be accurate in life, but you *create* with the voice of your spirit! Words ARE important. Accurate Words bring Accurate results- But I've learned it's not always the accuracy of the Word, but the power of the spirit that pushes that Word that makes things happen! It's one thing to have an iron ball, but it's another thing to have it explode out of a cannon! We want our spirit to be so strong that when God gives us a Word, our spirits can pick it up and propel it with our voice with such a force to break down any walls or obstacles that would stand against it. Power is a vehicle for love to be expressed, and the voice is the vehicle for a spirit to be expressed.

T.L. Osborn had said a unique saying- *"The power of the gospel is in its announcement"* What does that mean? Doesn't the gospel of Christ contain the power of God -as Romans 1:16 says? It is the power of God to those *who believe.* It takes a gospel spoken with a spirit of faith that can impregnate a person with faith to access God's Grace. (1Cor.4:12; Acts14:9-10)

T.L. Osborn learned that to have results standing before 10-100s of thousands, he had to release the Word at such a temperature and push with the strength of his spirit to announce the greatest gospel that creates healings, salvations, and so demons know that they dealing with an ambassador from heaven. Paul also emphasizes this later in Ephesians. *"Pray that I may speak the Word <u>boldly</u> <u>as I ought to</u> speak"*(Eph6:19-20) He taught his leadership the same- *"rebuke with all authority"* (Titus 2:15) Jesus stunned the crowds because of HOW He spoke, not just *what* He said! He spoke *"as one who had authority"*. They said 'no one ever spoke like this man.' Because He didn't speak AS a man. He spoke as God Himself would say it! Listen- they knew WHAT God spoke- the Bible- just like us. But HOW does He say it? That is often the missing ingredient.

These verses from Jeremiah 23:28-29 will be a great help to us in this matter. When we determine to speak His Words that we have with faith (faith-fully), we must know that God will ignite our spirits with fire so those Words will burn like napalm against anything contrary to them. In the same way, our voice can be used as a sledgehammer to deliver a word that impacts for all eternity. It will be great when our voice will be used so that we do not just give information, but literally create change. Our spirits can increase in strength so this will happen wherever we release this strength of our spirit through our voice.

One step further is that our voice can increase in strength so greatly that life begins to break out. Even the dead shall hear the voice from your nature as a son of God, <u>and</u> <u>shall</u> <u>live</u>. The way I picture it would be as a vocal defibrillator that delivers a powerful electrical shock through the vehicle of the voice which jumpstarts life into the person or situation. John Lake had the view that the power of the Spirit of God moves very similarly to the nature of electricity. This electricity has always existed, but simply needed to be generated and channeled effectively/efficiently.

This is where we stand as well as we look at all of the spiritual history of how God worked through mankind. There are no 'good old days' where the Spirit was really moving… there was simply a people who knew how to generate and channel the eternal River of the Spirit of God. There is no lack to the Spirit we have inside today as well, it just needs to be generated by our faith and actions with a imagination-filled determination. We should learn from history of what has been done, and build on it to create another revolution just like how the technological revolution built upon the achievements of the previous industrial revolution. Great strength in our spirit and voice is available, we just need to have a vivid consciousness of what we are really doing for this level of spiritual breakthrough to manifest through us.

**Challenge Questions:**

In believing and expecting this spiritual breakthrough dimension of receiving a greater strength of spirit and voice, note situations where you have experienced:

An enlargement of your voice with fresh impact, having a consciousness of your voice creating, shaping, establishing, and bringing the dead back to life.
(Isa.40:9, Isa.51:6)

1._____
_____
_____
_____

2._____
_____
_____
_____

3._____
_____
_____
_____

**A fresh conscious boldness in your voice, due to your request and expectation for it.**

1._____
_____
_____
_____

2._____
_____
_____
_____

3._____
_____
_____
_____

<u>Having an activated, highly-energized spirit;</u>
<u>Your spirit is buoyant, intense and passionate,</u>
<u>Able to rise quickly in every circumstance.</u>
<u>Never staying down because of this buoyancy.</u>
<u>HIGH JOY!</u>
<u>Victory and Dominion pulsating within your spirit!</u>

"Arise, shine; For your light has come! And the glory of the LORD is risen upon you. For behold the darkness shall cover the earth, and deep darkness the people; BUT the LORD will arise over you, and His glory will be SEEN upon you. The Gentiles shall come to your light, and kings to the brightness of your rising." (Isa.60:1-3)

## What This Means:

In Peter it says 'as newborn babes, desire the sincere milk of the Word, that you may grow thereby.' For this reason, spiritual hunger and thirst is necessary. Our spirit is complete in Christ, and now must be fed so it can grow and mature to manifest in specific ways according to the Word. In **Spirit Life Training** I gave six specific ways to feed, exercise and build one's spirit. When the spirit is strong, it becomes normal for your spirit to be released in powerful ways on a daily basis.

This is the point we want to come to. This is where our focus goes beyond continually feeding and maintaining your spirit as a pet, or like a child that needs to be sat down for a scheduled feeding. Of course this discipline is foundational, and until it is established, we can proceed no further. But there is a time when any discipline or habit, will take on a life of its own and instead of you scheduling your habit, your habit schedules you! When our spirit grows and matures to where it has an abundant life that overflows and feeds itself, as well as those around you. It becomes a continual cycle that floods you with spiritual energy, which propels you to obey God's Word, which feeds your spirit even more, which produces more of the expression of the Word and manifestation of the Spirit of God, and your spirit is again fed and built up... and the cycle continues to build momentum.

What a wonderful position to be in! At this point- who could possibly keep your spirit down? It is like someone pushing an inflated beach ball under the water. There is an irresistible pressure that is forcing it to rise upwards –one way or another- that ball is coming up! And the further it is pushed down, the higher it will pop up out of the water!

Our spirits can develop that kind of buoyancy. The enemy could throw his worst at you, to try to put you six feet under, but *'But if the Spirit of Him who raised Jesus from the dead dwells in you, He who raised Christ from the dead will also give life to your mortal bodies through His Spirit Who dwells in you'*(Rom.8:11) and you come up stronger than ever before. You just can't help it- this spirit that lives in you won't let you stay down. You can come to a point where you don't have to stir up the gift of God, the gift of God stirs you up! It is like Jeremiah when he said that 'His Word was like a fire in my bones, and he was weary of holding it back, in fact, he could not.' (Jer.20:9)

The only way to stop this river, is to make a deliberate choice of your Will to put on the parking brake and quench the spirit. It literally is like resisting temptation from the opposite end of the spectrum- you are resisting the spirit and life of God from breaking out to release God's goodness and energize your obedience.

All that goes to show, is the way one's spirit can become a dynamo of perpetual life and energy. This is truly the 'Spirit-filled' life. There is an autoimmune response to any negativity and depression. Your joy is contagious. Not because you are silly or have a great sense of humor, but you have a victory-based mindset because of this unshakable faith that God lives in you and delights to make you an overcomer like Himself. This joy also springs from a freedom that your spirit enjoys. Your inner security lets you be free to love, immune from intimidation, and prepared for adventure!

Our spirit is not static. It has a life and nature of its own. Like your own heart pumps the blood that keeps itself healthy and strong, your spirit pulsates with the joy of victory and a sense of dominion that produces an environment that gives your spirit the ability to resource itself. It can kick into high gear when your body is tired, and your emotions are stretched out of shape. Like a runner gets a second wind, or a second tank of gas is unlocked and accessed, your energy is restored, and your emotions are clarified. Your thoughts become clear, even when others around you are still trapped in feelings of weakness and negativity. Your ability to make clear firm decisions, with the relentless energy to follow through with action, sets you apart as a leader that connects you with other leaders.

Gone are the days where the mercy of God has to massage you into action, but you have now installed a self-starting engine, and your spirit is building its own momentum in your life. Your light has come, and as you arise, the Lord rises upon you.

**Challenge Questions:**

In believing and expecting this spiritual breakthrough dimension of receiving an activated, buoyant and passionate spirit, note situations where you have experienced:

Your spirit kicking in an extra boost of strength, in the moment you needed it.

1._____
_____
_____
_____

2._____
_____
_____
_____

3._____
_____
_____
_____

A fresh consciousness of victory and dominion that floods your being -note the situations where it remains like this for an extended period of time.

1._____
_____
_____
_____

2._____
_____
_____
_____

3._____
_____
_____
_____

Areas where obedience to God's word has become more fluid because of this constant momentum of spiritual energy which directs you in this manner.

1._____

2._____

3._____

4._____

Thank you for investing your time and resources into this! We believe this handbook will be a great help to you for years to come.

Please visit our website at **www.spiritlifetraining.com** for more resources and information.

If you are interested in contacting/inviting Timothy Jorgensen for a ministry engagement, or a Spirit Life Training event in your area, please email us at spiritlifetraining@gmail.com with the details of your request.

Made in the USA
Lexington, KY
22 September 2018